First Facts™

The Solar System

Jupiter

by Adele Richardson

Consultant:
Stephen J. Kortenkamp, PhD
Research Scientist
Planetary Science Institute, Tucson, Arizona

Capstone press

Mankato, Minnesota

First Facts is published by Capstone Press,
151 Good Counsel Drive, P.O. Box 669, Mankato, Minnesota 56002.
www.capstonepress.com

Library of Congress Cataloging-in-Publication Data
Richardson, Adele, 1966–
    Jupiter / by Adele Richardson.
    p. cm.—(First facts. The solar system)
    Includes bibliographical references and index.
    ISBN 0-7368-3688-8 (hardcover)
    1. Jupiter (Planet)—Juvenile literature. I. Title. II. Series: First facts. The solar system.
QB661.R54 2005
523.45—dc22   2004011049

Summary: Discusses the orbit, atmosphere, and exploration of the planet Jupiter.

Editorial Credits
Christopher Harbo, editor; Juliette Peters, designer and illustrator; Jo Miller, photo researcher;
    Scott Thoms, photo editor

Photo Credits
NASA/JPL, 14
Photodisc, 1, 4, 16–17, planet images within illustrations and chart, 6–7, 11, 13, 19, 21
Photo Researchers Inc./Science Photo Library/NASA, cover, 9; Space Telescope Science
    Institute/NASA, 16 (inset)
Space Images/NASA/JPL, 5, 8, 15, 20

1 2 3 4 5 6 10 09 08 07 06 05

Table of Contents

Voyager 1 Visits Jupiter

In 1979, *Voyager 1* became the third spacecraft to fly by Jupiter. Pictures from *Voyager 1* showed thin rings around Jupiter. No one had ever seen them before. These pictures taught scientists more about the solar system's largest planet.

Fast Facts about Jupiter
Diameter: 88,750 miles (143,000 kilometers)
Average Distance from Sun: 483 million miles (777 million kilometers)
Average Temperature (cloud top): minus 163 degrees Fahrenheit (minus 108 degrees Celsius)
Length of Day: 9 hours, 55 minutes
Length of Year: 11 Earth years, 11 months
Moons: at least 63
Rings: 3

The Solar System

Jupiter is the fifth planet from the Sun. It is one of the gas giants, along with Saturn, Uranus, and Neptune. Pluto is the farthest planet from the Sun. It is made of rock and ice. The four planets closest to the Sun are rocky. They are Mercury, Venus, Earth, and Mars.

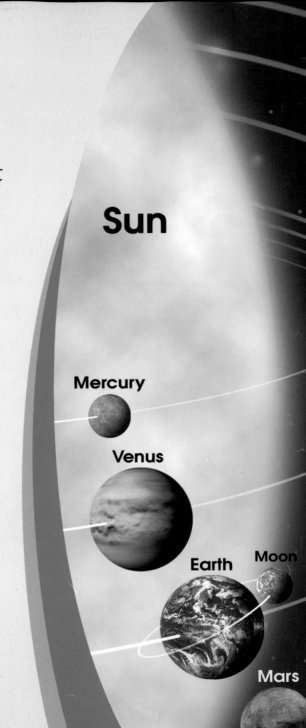

Sun

Mercury

Venus

Earth

Moon

Mars

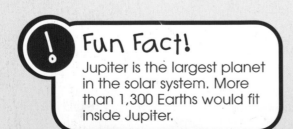

Fun Fact!
Jupiter is the largest planet in the solar system. More than 1,300 Earths would fit inside Jupiter.

Jupiter

Saturn

Uranus

Pluto

Neptune

Jupiter's Atmosphere

The gases surrounding a planet are called its **atmosphere**. Jupiter has a thick, cloudy atmosphere. It is mostly made of **hydrogen** gas.

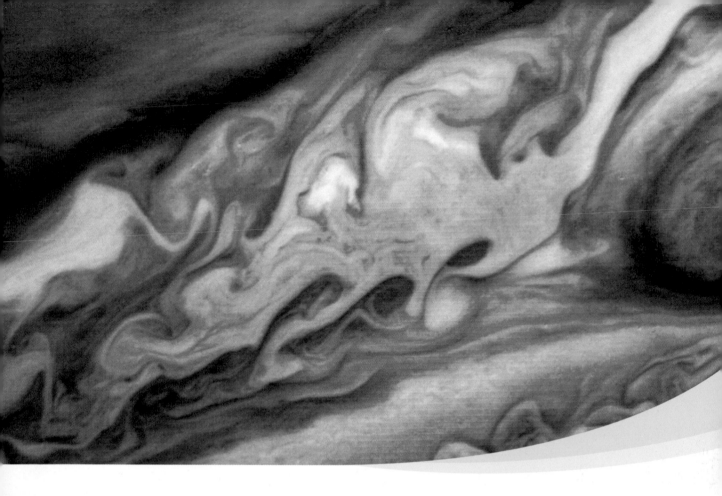

Clouds move quickly around Jupiter.
Winds blow the clouds faster than
400 miles (640 kilometers) per hour.

Jupiter's Makeup

Jupiter does not have a solid surface. A thick atmosphere of gases and ice pushes down on the planet's center. This pushing force is called **pressure**. The pressure makes gases deep inside Jupiter hot and thick, like syrup. A rocky **core** may lie in the planet's center.

Fun Fact!
Jupiter's pressure and heat crush and melt any spacecraft that enters its clouds.

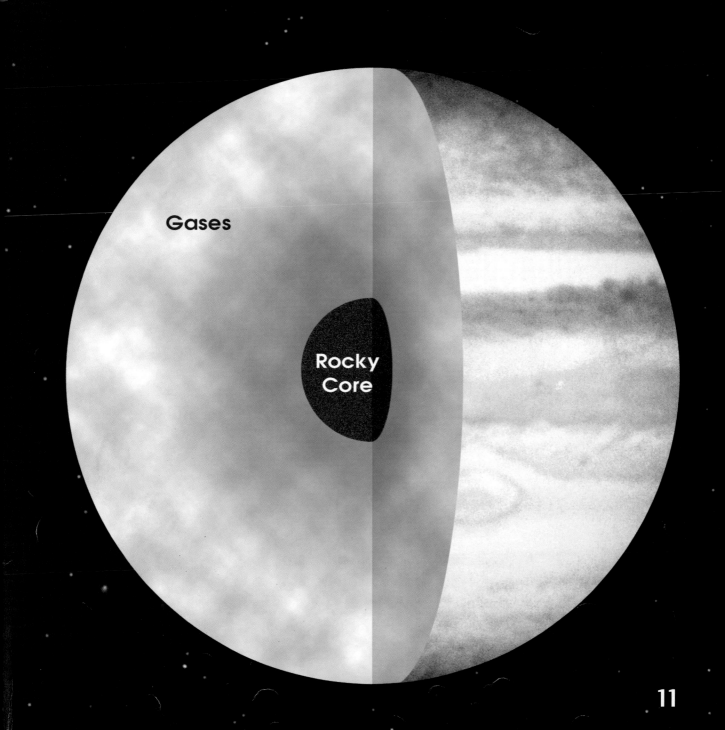

Gases

Rocky
Core

How Jupiter Moves

Jupiter spins quickly on its **axis** as it moves around the Sun. The giant planet takes 9 hours and 55 minutes to spin on its axis once. Jupiter moves around the Sun very slowly. The planet takes almost 12 Earth years to circle the Sun one time.

Fact!
The farther a planet is from the Sun, the longer it takes the planet to go around it.

Sun

Path around the Sun

Jupiter

Axis

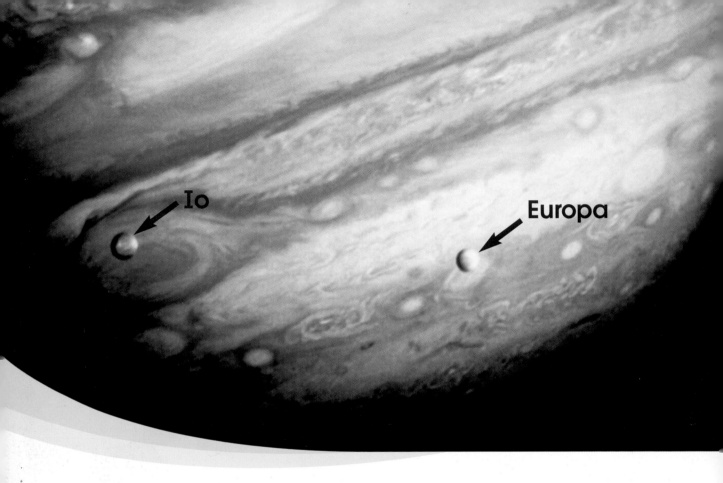

Io

Europa

Moons and Rings

Jupiter has at least 63 moons. The
moon Io has volcanoes that erupt hot
lava. The moon Europa may have an
ocean under its icy surface.

Jupiter has three rings. The rings are made of dust and pieces of rock. The rings are thin and faint. Scientists use special cameras to see them.

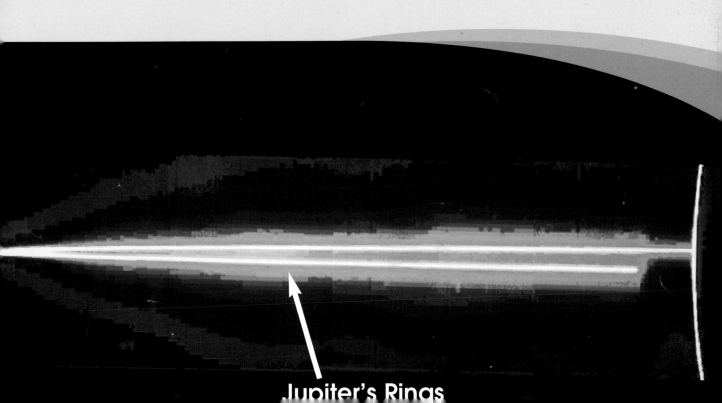

Jupiter's Rings

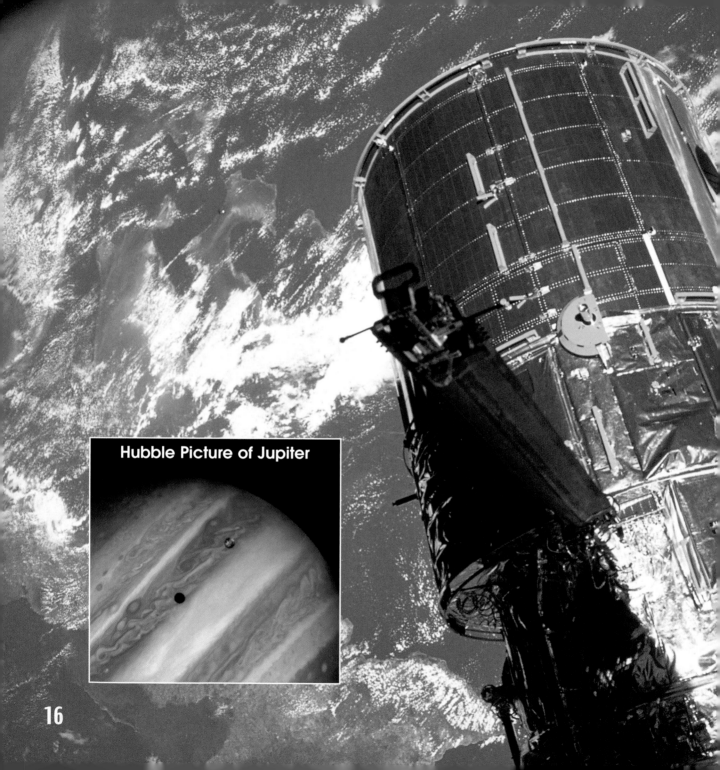

Hubble Picture of Jupiter

Studying Jupiter

Jupiter is studied with spacecraft and **telescopes**. Seven spacecraft have visited the planet. From Earth, people study Jupiter with telescopes. Some of the clearest pictures of Jupiter are taken with the Hubble Space Telescope.

! Fun Fact!
The Hubble Space Telescope is the size of a school bus.

Comparing Jupiter to Earth

Jupiter and Earth are very different. Earth is made of rock. Jupiter is made of ice and gases. People could not breathe the air on Jupiter. The planet does not have a surface to walk on. People will keep studying the planet with spacecraft and telescopes.

Fun Fact!

Jupiter's moon Io is about the same size as Earth's moon.

Size Comparison

Jupiter

 Earth

Amazing but True!

Jupiter's Great Red Spot is the biggest storm in the solar system. Almost three Earths could fit inside it. The Great Red Spot is like a huge hurricane on Earth. The giant storm has been raging on Jupiter for more than 350 years.

Planet Comparison Chart

Planet	Size Rank (1=largest)	Makeup	1 Trip around the Sun (Earth Time)
Mercury	8	rock	88 days
Venus	6	rock	225 days
Earth	5	rock	365 days, 6 hours
Mars	7	rock	687 days
Jupiter	1	gases and ice	11 years, 11 months
Saturn	2	gases and ice	29 years, 6 months
Uranus	3	gases and ice	84 years
Neptune	4	gases and ice	164 years, 10 months
Pluto	9	rock and ice	248 years

Glossary

atmosphere (AT-muhss-feehr)—the mixture of gases that surrounds some planets and moons

axis (AK-siss)—an imaginary line that runs through the middle of a planet; a planet spins on its axis.

core (KOR)—the inner part of a planet that is made of metal or rock

hydrogen (HYE-druh-juhn)—a colorless gas that is lighter than air and burns easily

pressure (PRESH-ur)—the force produced by pressing on something

telescope (TEL-uh-skope)—an instrument that makes faraway objects appear larger and closer

Read More

Goss, Tim. *Jupiter.* The Universe. Chicago: Heinemann Library, 2003.

Rau, Dana Meachen. *Jupiter.* Our Solar System. Minneapolis: Compass Point Books, 2002.

Young, Abby. *Jupiter.* The Library of the Nine Planets. New York: Rosen, 2005.

Internet Sites

FactHound offers a safe, fun way to find Internet sites related to this book. All of the sites on FactHound have been researched by our staff.

Here's how:
1. Visit *www.facthound.com*
2. Type in this special code **0736836888** for age-appropriate sites. Or enter a search word related to this book for a more general search.
3. Click on the **Fetch It** button.

FactHound will fetch the best sites for you!

Index